POP/ROCK
LOVE SONGS

D1441462

CONTENTS

Always

Words and Music by
Jon Bon Jovi

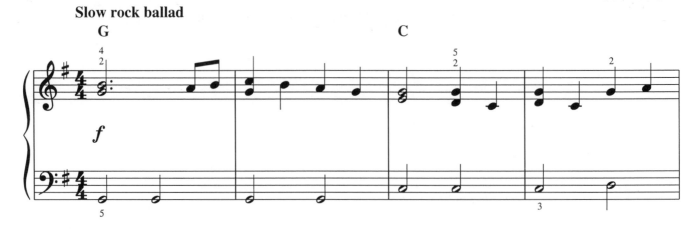

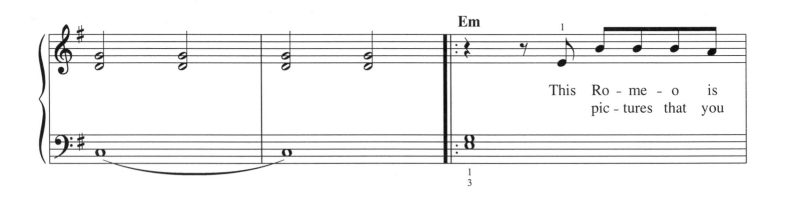

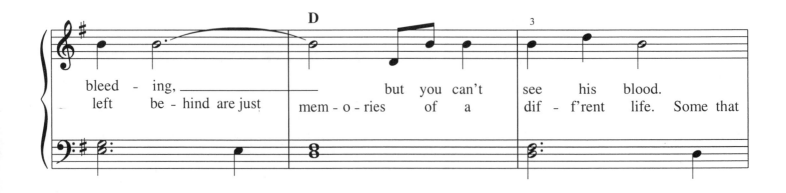

Copyright © 1994 PolyGram International Publishing, Inc. and Bon Jovi Publishing
International Copyright Secured   All Rights Reserved

It's noth-ing but some feel - ings ____ that this old dog kicked
made us laugh, some that made us cry, one that made you have to

up.
say good - bye. What I'd give to run my fin - gers through your

It's been rain - ing since you left me, now I'm
hair, to

drown - ing ____ in the flood. ____
touch your ____ lips, to hold you near.

You see, I've al - ways been a
When you say your prayers try to

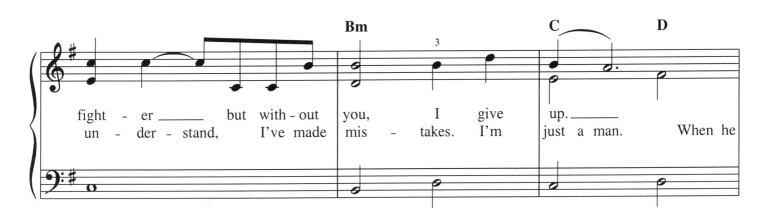

fight - er ____ but with - out you, I give up. ____
un - der - stand, I've made mis - takes. I'm just a man. When he

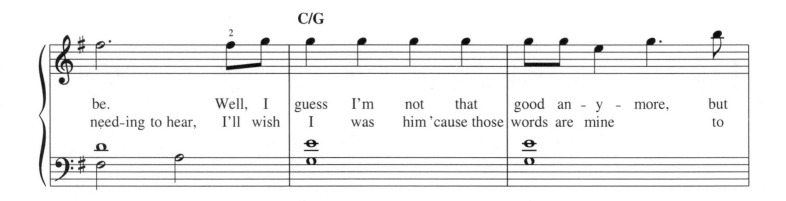

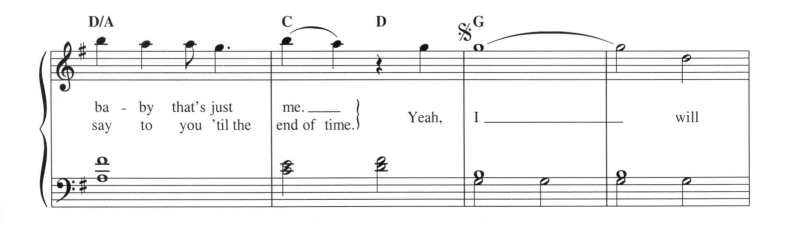

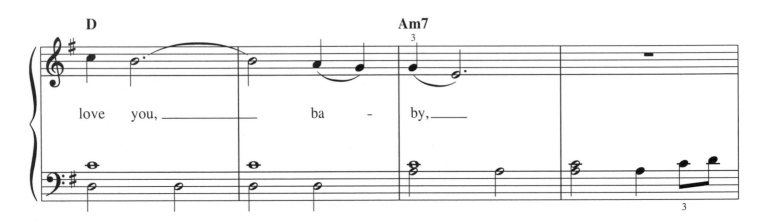

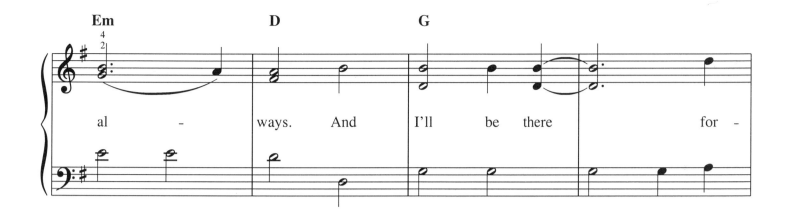

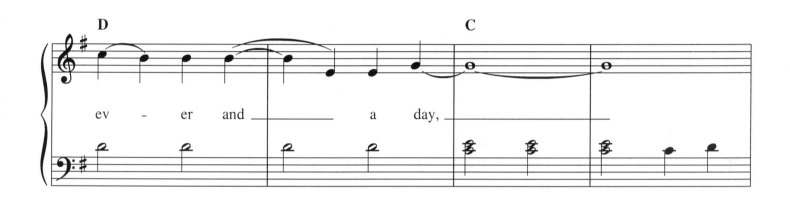

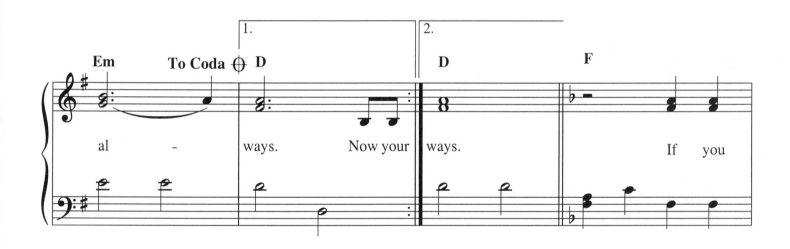

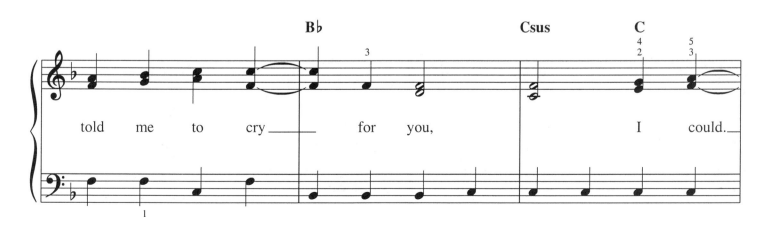

If you told me to die for you

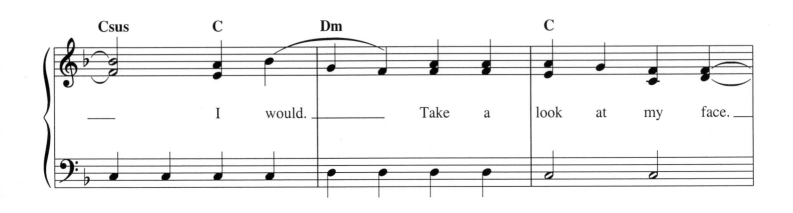

I would. Take a look at my face.

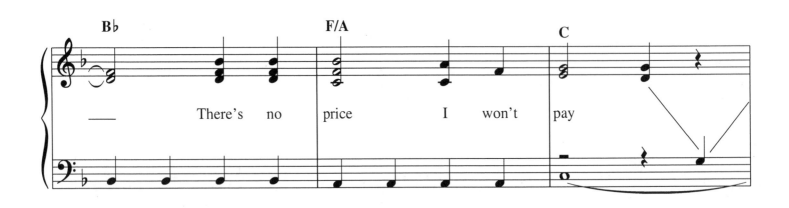

There's no price I won't pay

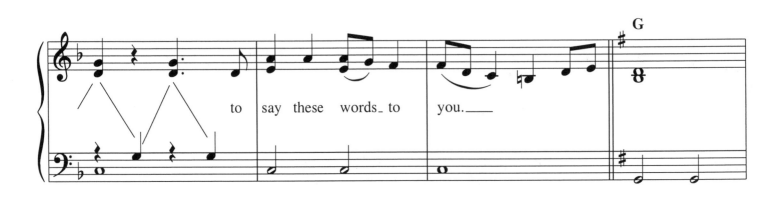

to say these words to you.

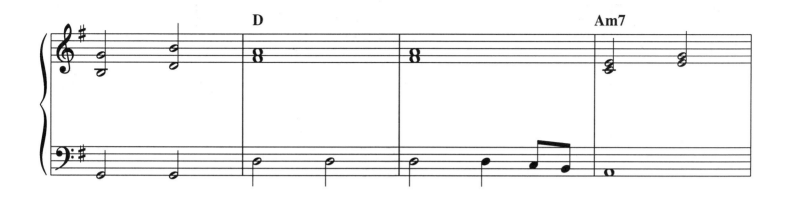

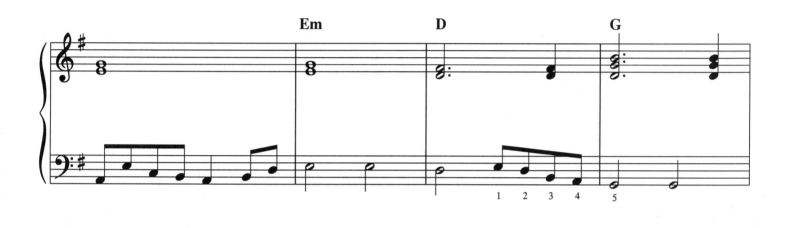

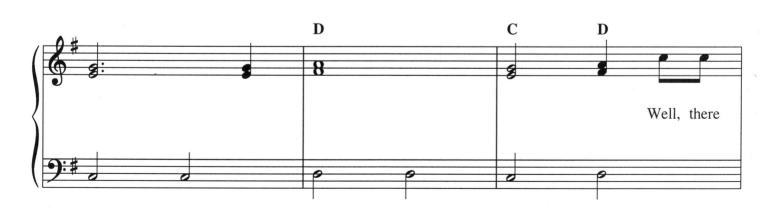

Well, there

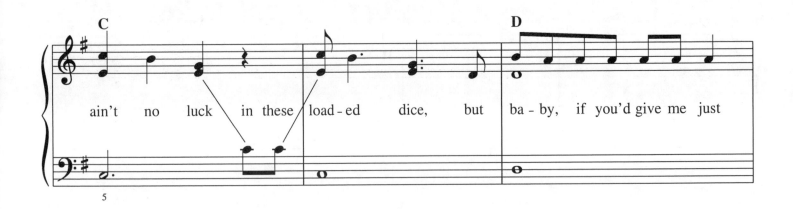

ain't no luck in these load-ed dice, but ba - by, if you'd give me just

one more try we can pack up our old dreams and our old lives. We'll

find a place ___ where the sun still shines yeah. ___

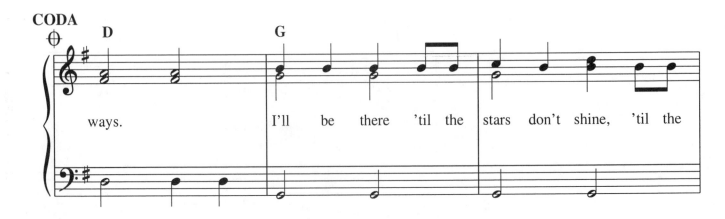

ways. I'll be there 'til the stars don't shine, 'til the

heav-ens burst and the words don't rhyme. I know when I die you'll be

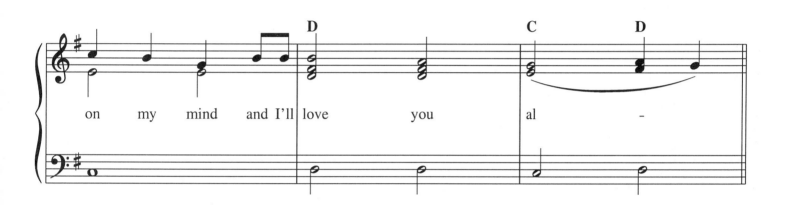

on my mind and I'll love you al -

ways.

Repeat and Fade

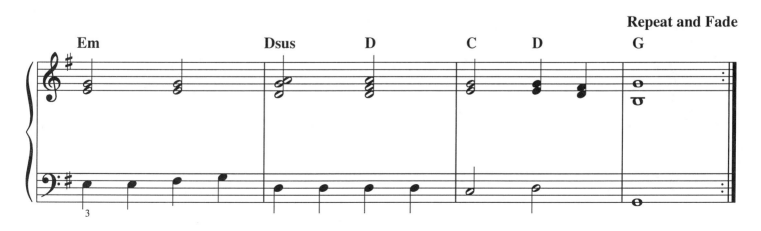

Annie's Song

Words and Music by
John Denver

Copyright © 1974 Cherry Lane Music Publishing Company, Inc. (ASCAP) and DreamWorks Songs (ASCAP)
Worldwide Rights for DreamWorks Songs Administered by Cherry Lane Music Publishing Company, Inc.
International Copyright Secured   All Rights Reserved

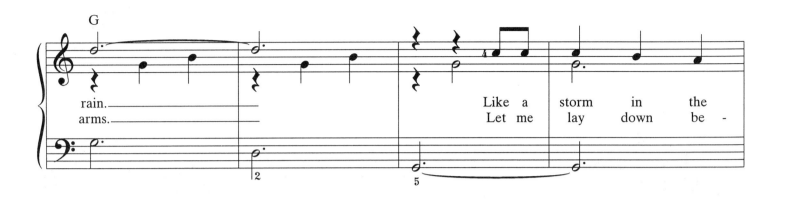

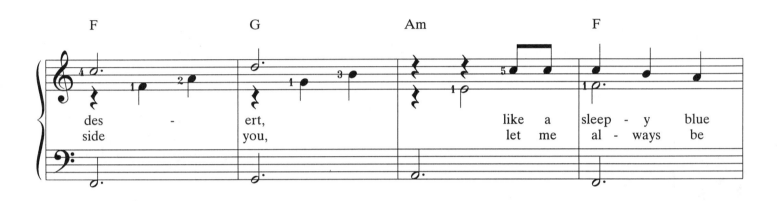

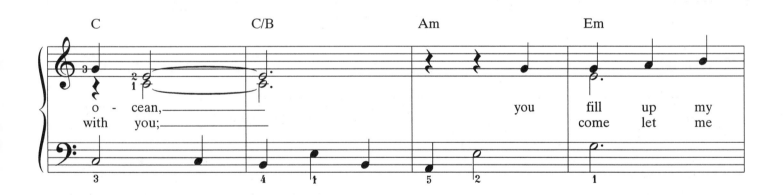

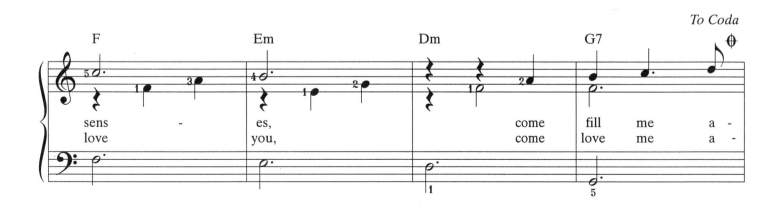

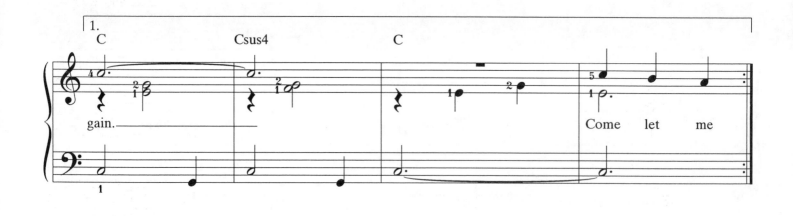

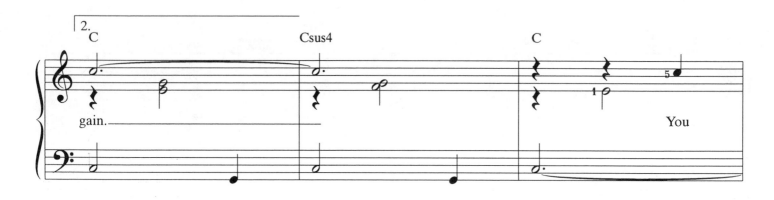

Bed of Roses

Words and Music by
Jon Bon Jovi

Moderately slow

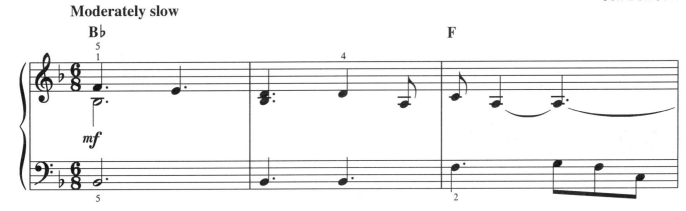

Copyright © 1992 PolyGram International Publishing, Inc. and Bon Jovi Publishing
International Copyright Secured   All Rights Reserved

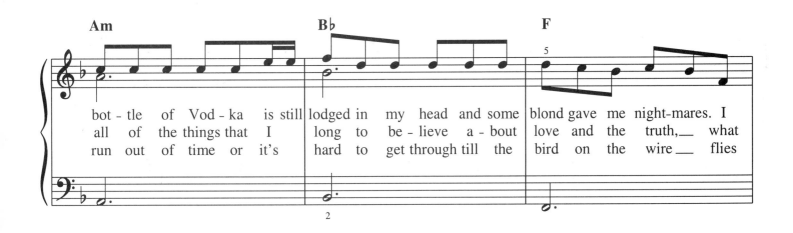

bot-tle of Vod-ka is still lodged in my head and some blond gave me night-mares. I
all of the things that I long to be-lieve a-bout love and the truth,___ what
run out of time or it's hard to get through till the bird on the wire ___ flies

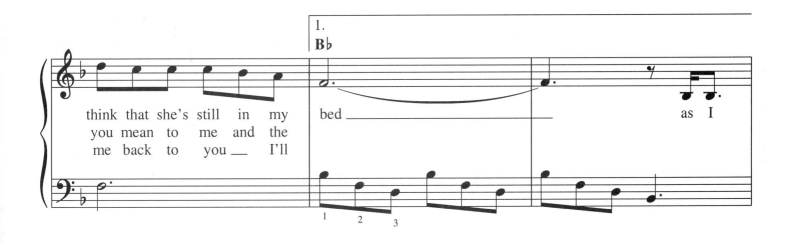

think that she's still in my bed ___ as I
you mean to me and the
me back to you ___ I'll

dream a-bout mo-vies they won't make of me when I'm dead.___ With an

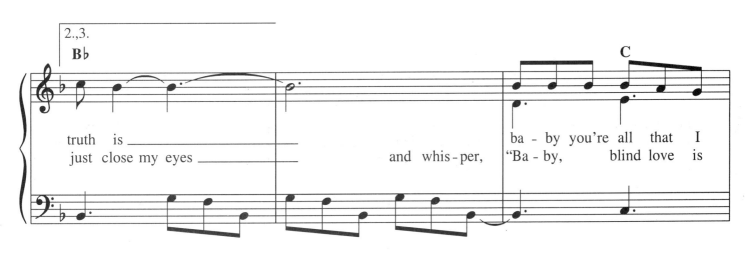

truth is ___
just close my eyes ___ and whis-per, ba-by you're all that I
"Ba-by, blind love is

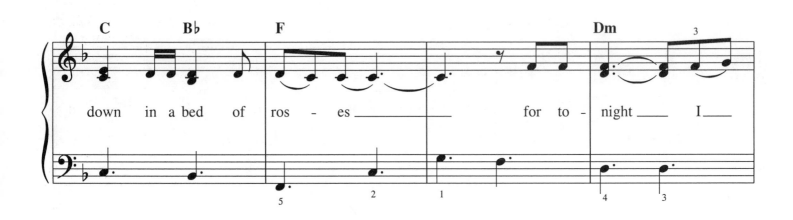

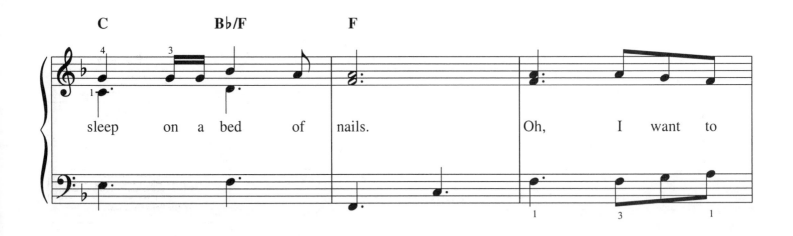

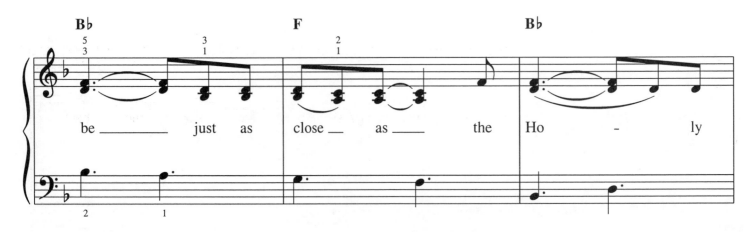

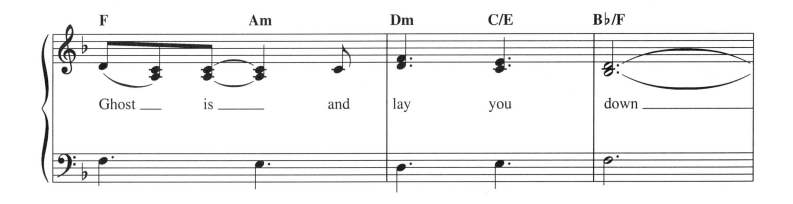

Ghost ____ is _____ and lay you down _____

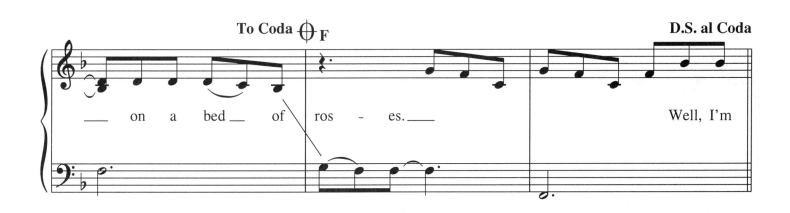

To Coda ⊕ **F**   **D.S. al Coda**

____ on a bed __ of ros - es. ____ Well, I'm

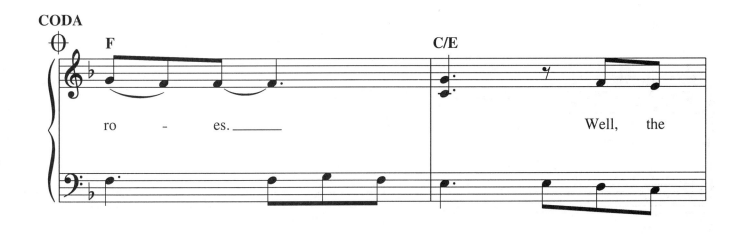

CODA

ro - es. ____ Well, the

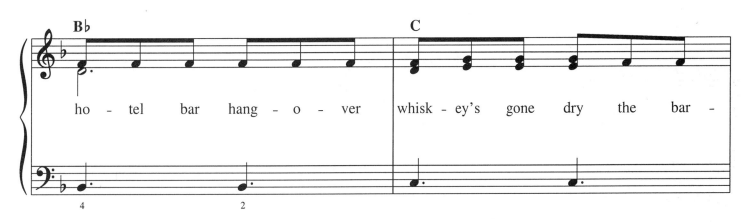

ho - tel bar hang - o - ver whisk - ey's gone dry the bar -

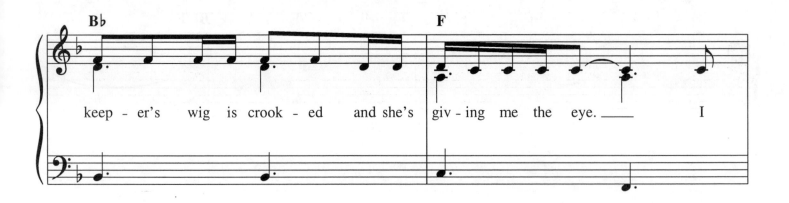

keep - er's   wig   is   crook - ed   and she's   giv - ing   me   the   eye. _____   I

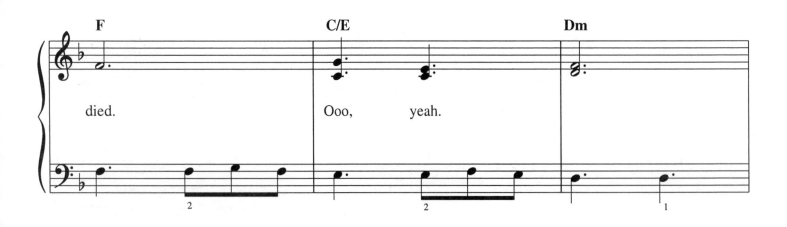

might have   said   yeah, _____   but   I   laughed so   hard   I   think   I

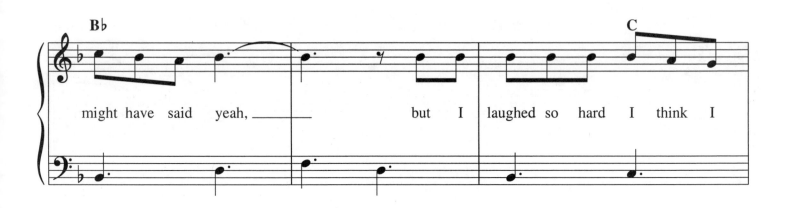

died.   Ooo,   yeah.

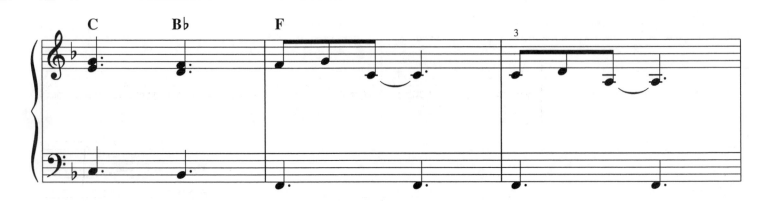

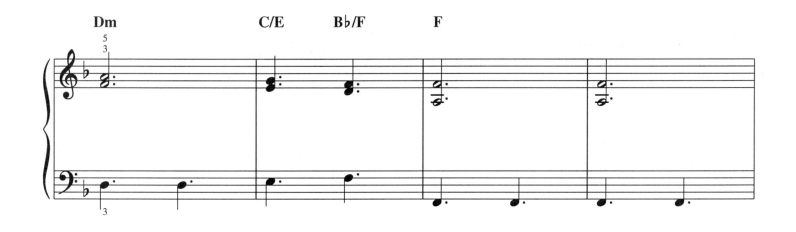

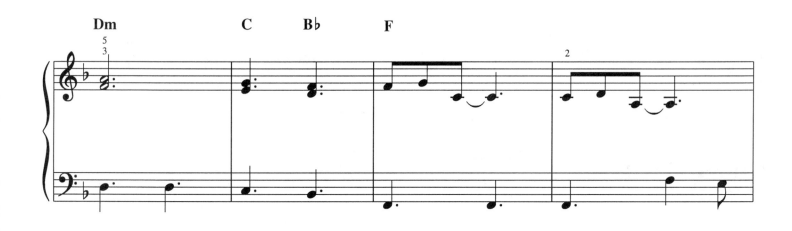

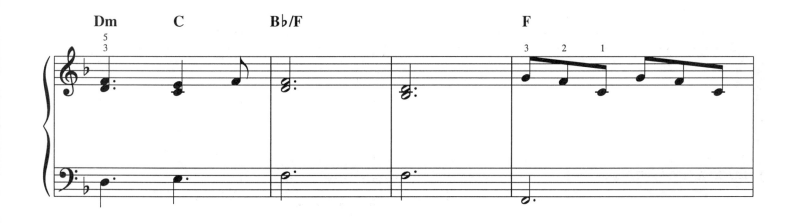

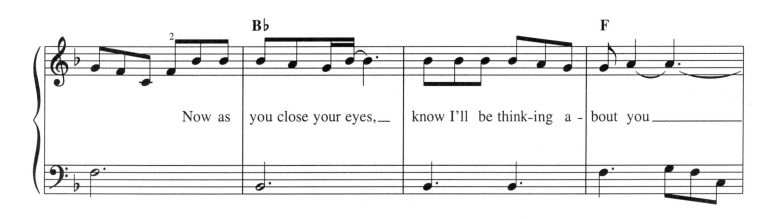

Now as   you close your eyes,__   know I'll be think-ing a - bout you____

while my | mis-tress, she calls me to | stand in her spot-light ___ | a-gain. ___

___ To-night, I | won't be a lone ___ but you | know that don't mean I'm not | lone-ly ___

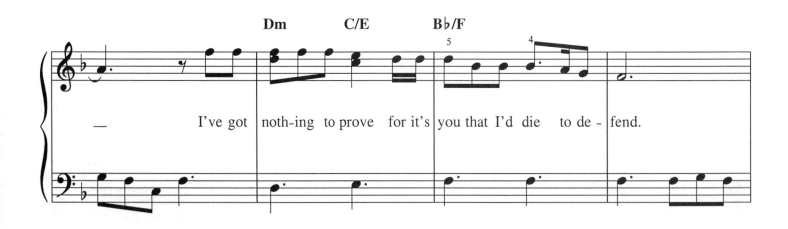

___ I've got | noth-ing to prove for it's | you that I'd die to de - | fend.

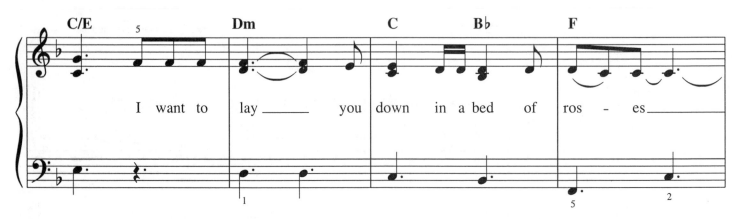

I want to | lay ___ you | down in a bed of | ros - es ___

22

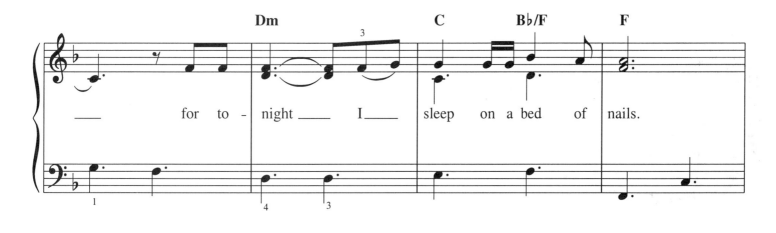

for to - night _____ I _____ sleep on a bed of nails.

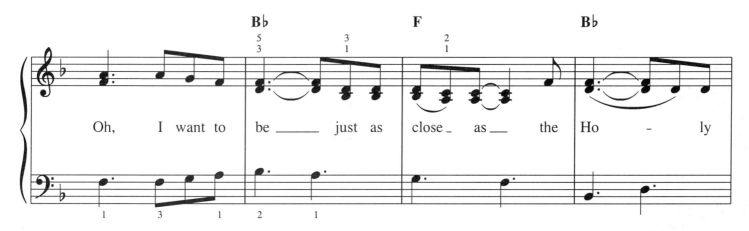

Oh, I want to be _____ just as close _ as _ the Ho - ly

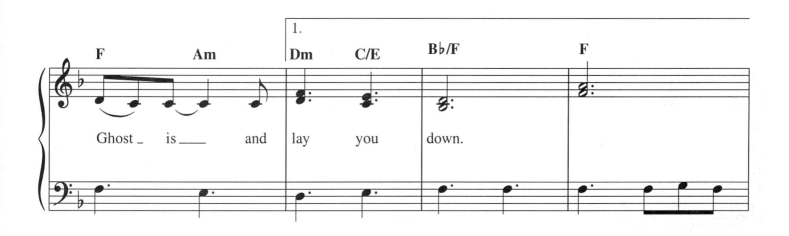

Ghost _ is _ and lay you down.

I want to lay you down on a bed _ of ros - es. _

Butterfly Kisses

Words and Music by Randy Thomas
and Bob Carlisle

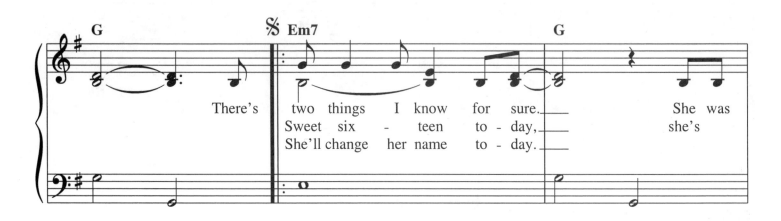

There's two things I know for sure.___ She was
Sweet six - teen to - day,___ she's
She'll change her name to - day.___

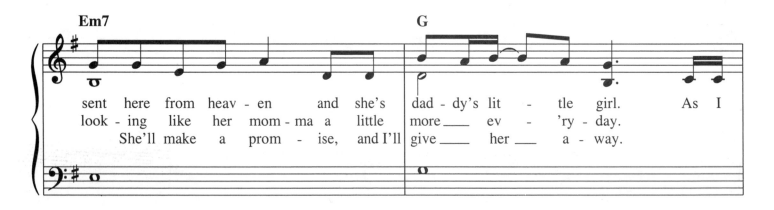

sent here from heav - en and she's dad - dy's lit - tle girl. As I
look - ing like her mom - ma a little more___ ev - 'ry - day.
She'll make a prom - ise, and I'll give ___ her ___ a - way.

drop to my knees ___ by her bed at night, ___ she talks to Je - sus, and
One part ___ wom - an, the oth - er part girl. To per - fume and make - up from
Stand - ing in the bride room just star - ing at her, she asked me what I'm think - ing and I

Copyright © 1996 PolyGram International Publishing, Inc. and Diadem Music Publishing
International Copyright Secured   All Rights Reserved

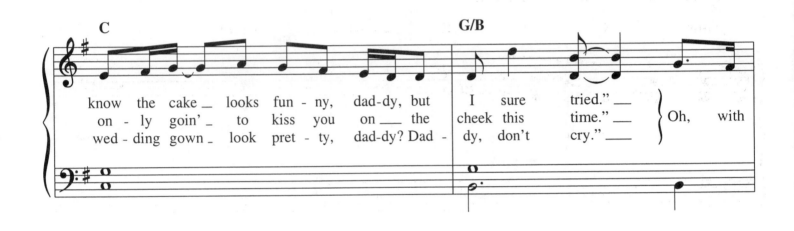

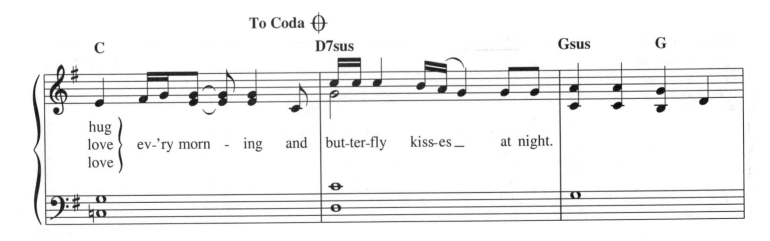

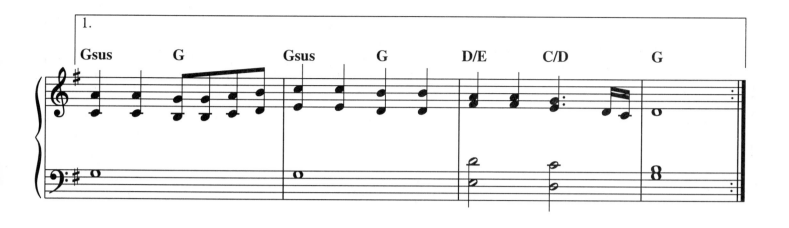

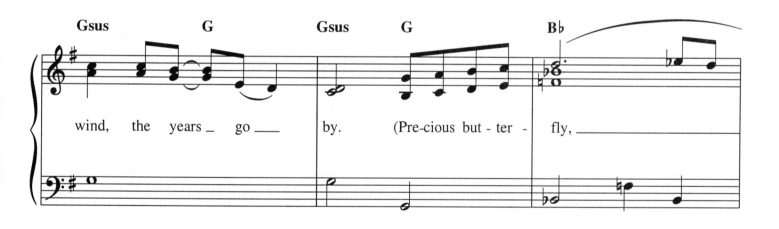

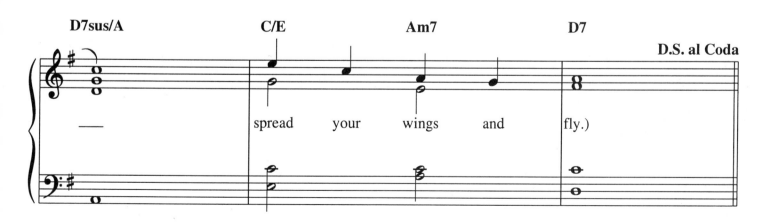

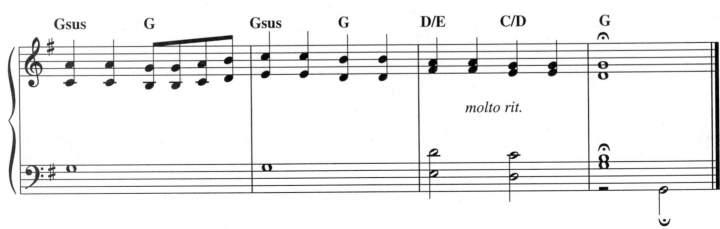

I Believe in You and Me

from the Touchstone Motion Picture THE PREACHER'S WIFE

Words and Music by David Wolfert
and Sandy Linzer

© 1981, 1982 EMI SOSAHA MUSIC INC., JONATHAN THREE MUSIC and LINZER MUSIC
All Rights Reserved   International Copyright Secured   Used by Permission

you will al - ways be the one for
Just to be right where you are, my

me. _____ Oh, yes, you will. And I be-lieve in
love. _____ You know I love you, boy. I'll nev - er

dreams a - gain. _____ I be-lieve that love will nev - er end. And
leave you out. _____ I will al - ways let you in, boy oh ba-by, to

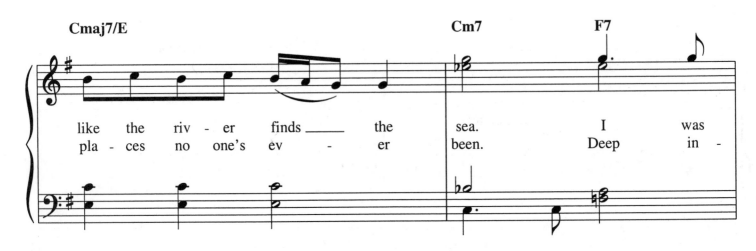

like the riv - er finds _____ the sea. I was
pla - ces no one's ev - er been. Deep in -

lost, _____ now I'm ____ free _____ 'cause
side, _____ can't you see _____ that

I be - lieve _ in you and me. I will nev - er
I be - lieve _ in you and

me. May - be I'm a fool _____ to

feel the way I do. _____ I would play the fool for - ev - er

just to be with you for - ev - er.

I be-lieve in

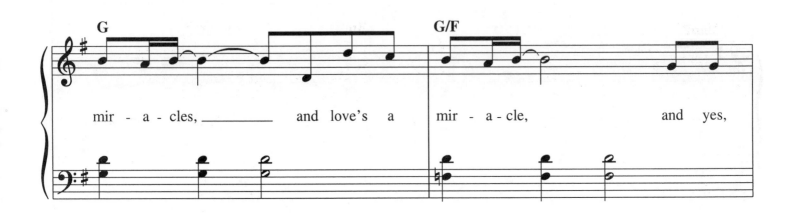

mir - a - cles, _____ and love's a

mir - a - cle, and yes,

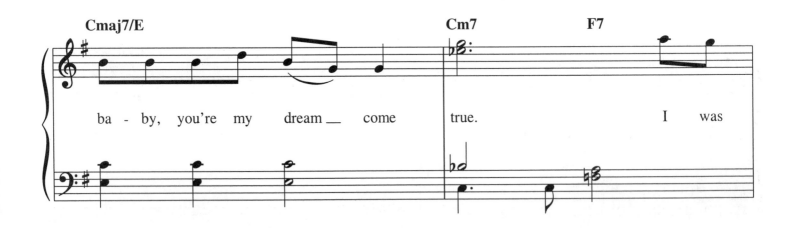

ba - by, you're my dream ___ come

true. I was

lost, _____ now I'm

free, _____ oh ba - by, 'cause

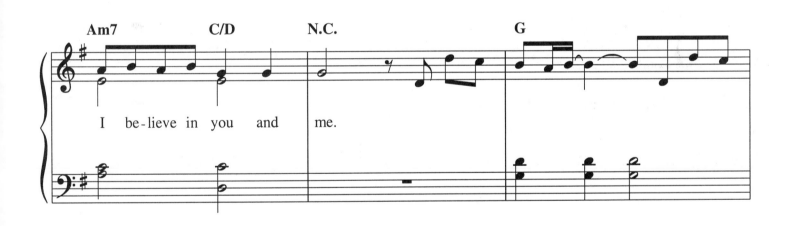

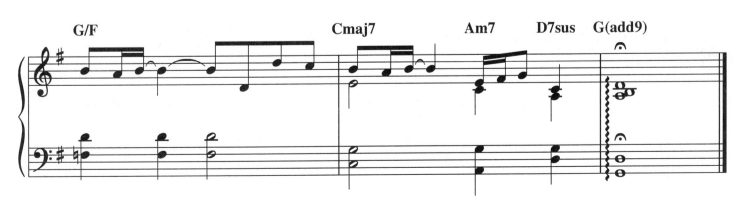

Can't Smile Without You

Words and Music by
Chris Arnold, David Martin and Geoff Morrow

Copyright © 1975 Dick James Music Limited
All Rights for the United States and Canada Administered by Songs Of PolyGram International, Inc.
International Copyright Secured   All Rights Reserved

feel sad when you're sad. I feel glad when

you're glad, If you only knew what I'm going through;

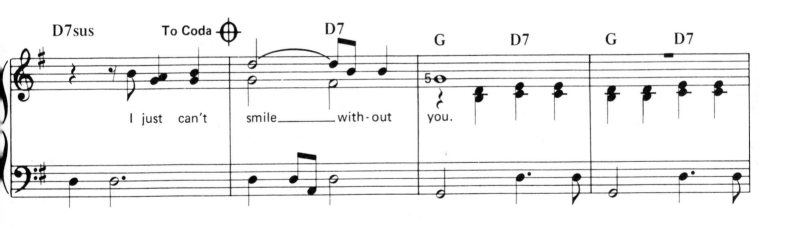

I just can't smile without you.

You come a - long just like a song and bright - ened my day.

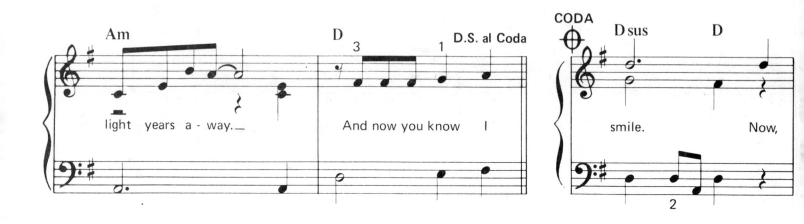

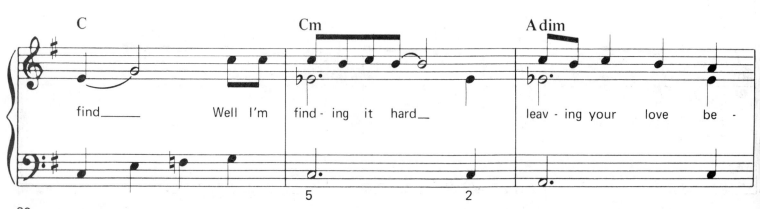

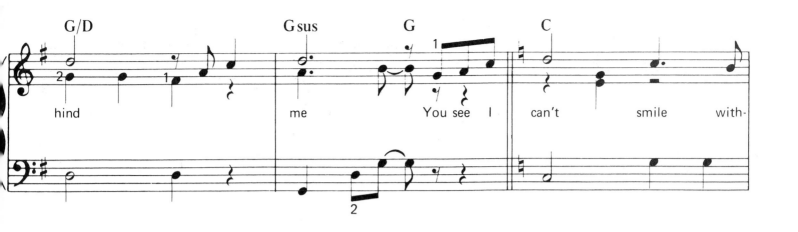

hind me You see I can't smile with-

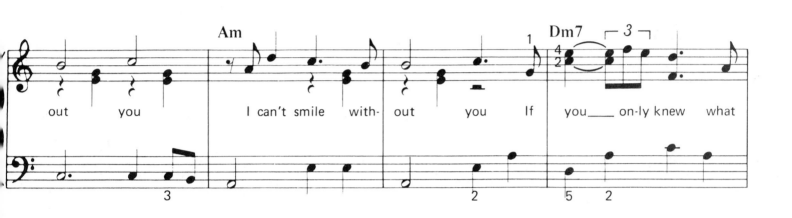

out you I can't smile with- out you If you___ on-ly knew what

I'm___go-ing through I just can't smile with-out you.___

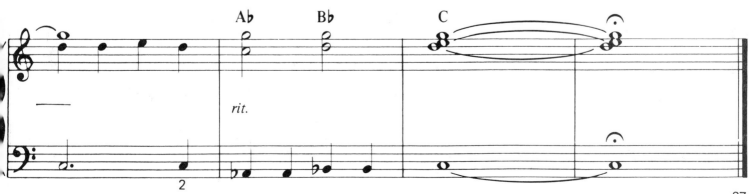

rit.

Follow Me

Words and Music by
John Denver

Moderately fast

It's by far the hard-est thing I've ev-er

done, to be so in love with

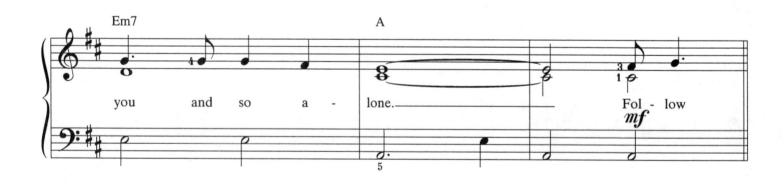

you and so a-lone. Fol-low

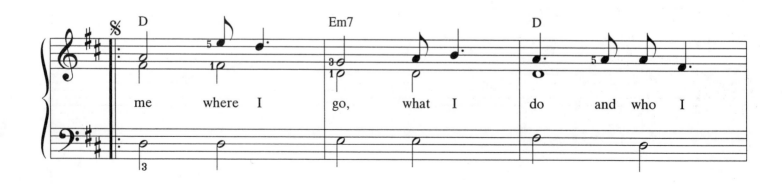

me where I go, what I do and who I

Copyright © 1969; Renewed 1997 Cherry Lane Music Publishing Company, Inc. (ASCAP) and DreamWorks Songs (ASCAP)
Worldwide Rights for DreamWorks Songs Administered by Cherry Lane Music Publishing Company, Inc.
International Copyright Secured   All Rights Reserved

know.———— Make it | part of you———— to | be a part of

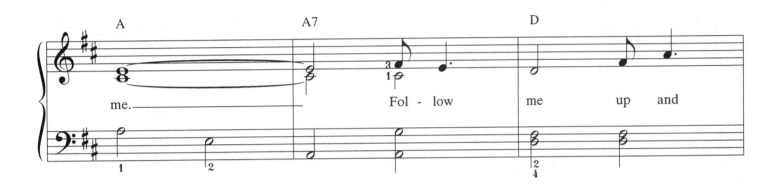

me.———————— | Fol - low | me up and

down, all——— the | way and all a - | round.

To Coda

Take my hand———— | and say you'll fol - low

me._____ It's long been on my
You see, I'd like to share my

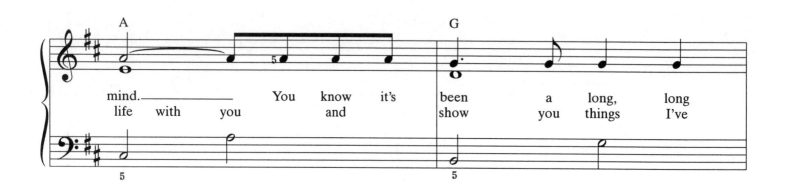

mind._____ You know it's been a long, long
life with you and show you things I've

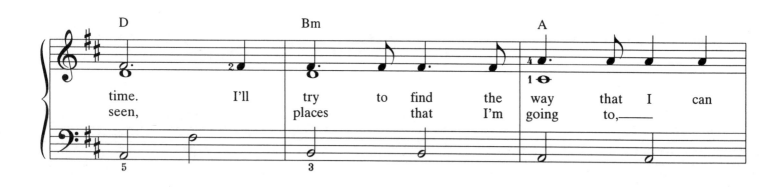

time. I'll try to find the way that I can
seen, places that I'm going to,____

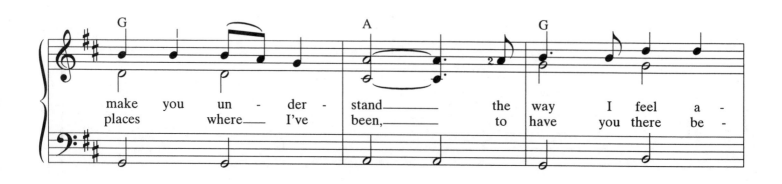

make you un- der- stand____ the way I feel a-
places where__ I've been,____ to have you there be-

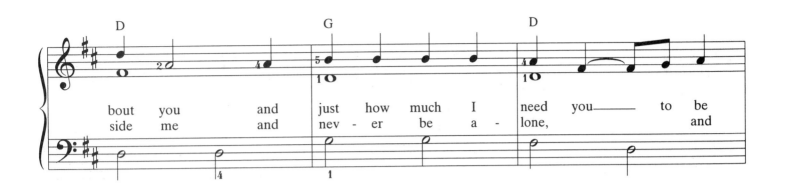

bout you   and   just   how   much   I   need   you_____   to   be
side me   and   nev - er   be   a -   lone,   and

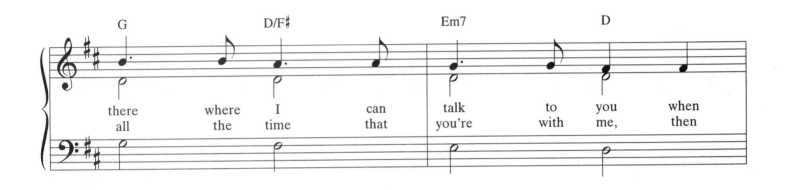

there   where   I   can   talk   to   you   when
all   the   time   that   you're   with   me,   then

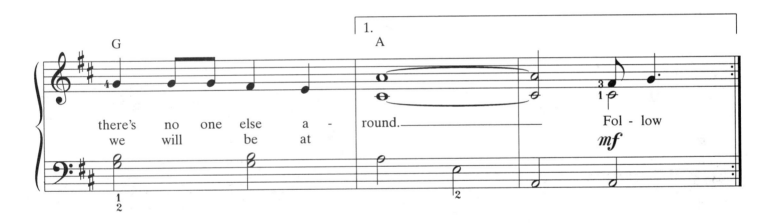

there's   no   one   else   a -   round._____   Fol - low
we   will   else   be   at   *mf*

home._____   Fol - low
mf

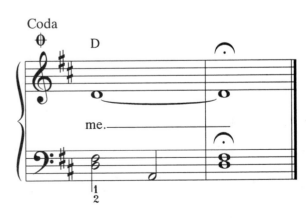

me._____

For All We Know
from the Motion Picture LOVERS AND OTHER STRANGERS

Words by Robb Wilson and James Griffin
Music by Fred Karlin

© Copyright 1970 by MCA MUSIC PUBLISHING, A Division of UNIVERSAL STUDIOS, INC.
Copyright Renewed
International Copyright Secured   All Rights Reserved

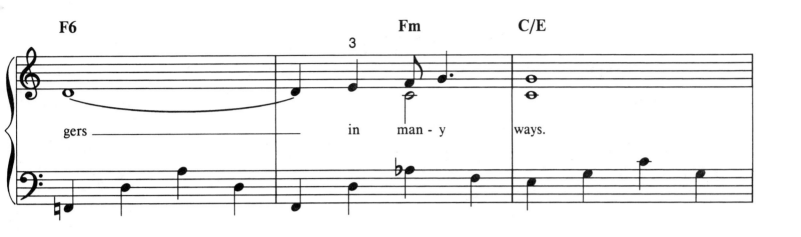

gers _____ in man - y ways.

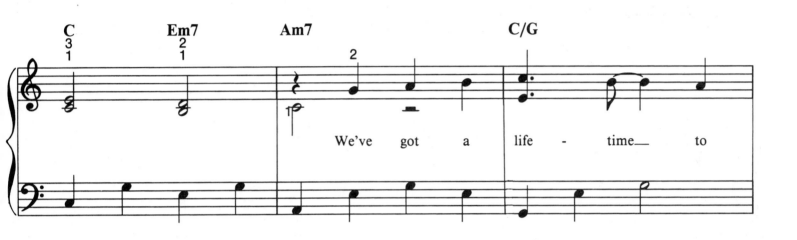

We've got a life - time__ to

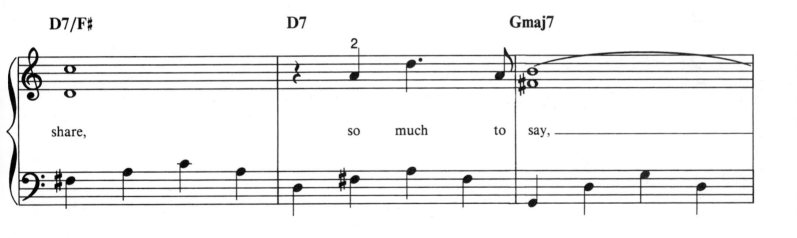

share, so much to say, _____

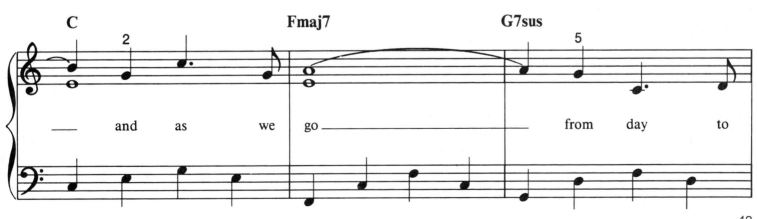

__ and as we go _____ from day to

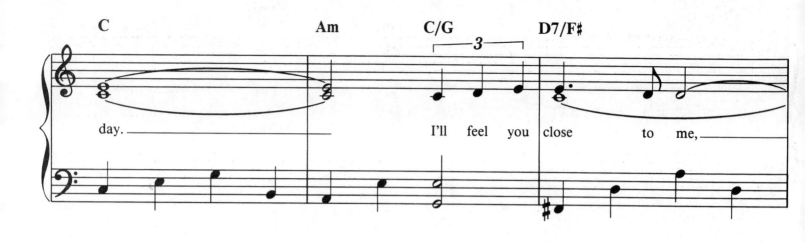

C   Am   C/G   D7/F#

day._____ I'll feel you close   to   me,_____

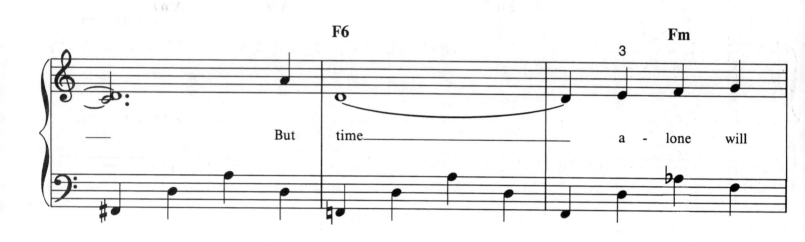

F6   Fm

__ But   time_____ a - lone will

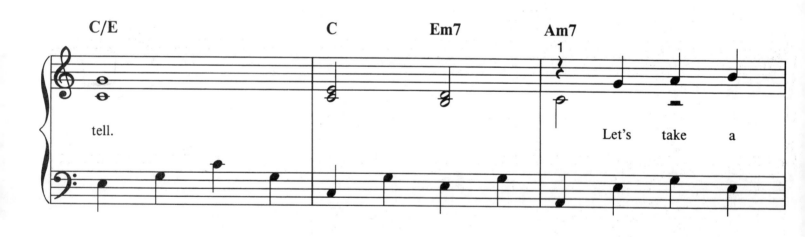

C/E   C   Em7   Am7

tell.   Let's take   a

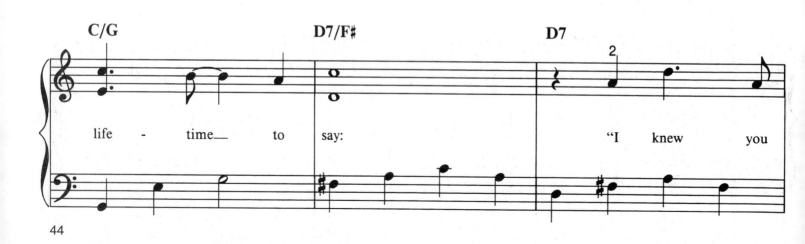

C/G   D7/F#   D7

life - time__ to say: "I   knew   you

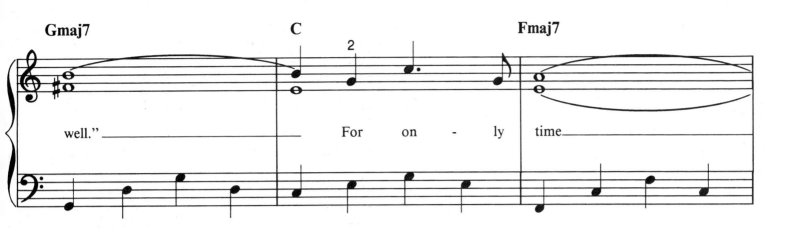

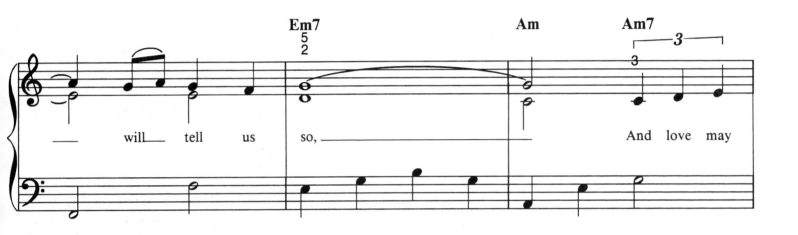

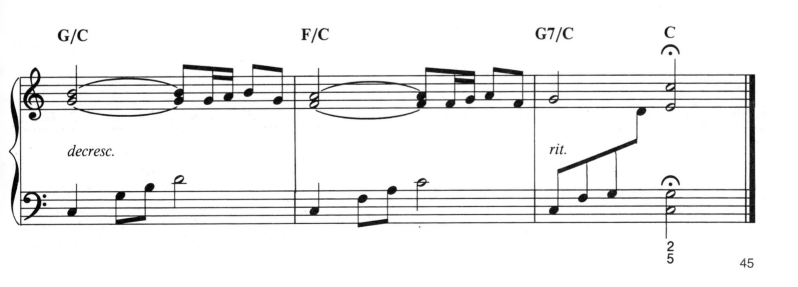

45

From This Moment On

Words and Music by Shania Twain
and R.J. Lange

Freely

mf (Spoken:) I do swear   (Sung:) that I'll   al - ways   be there.

With pedal

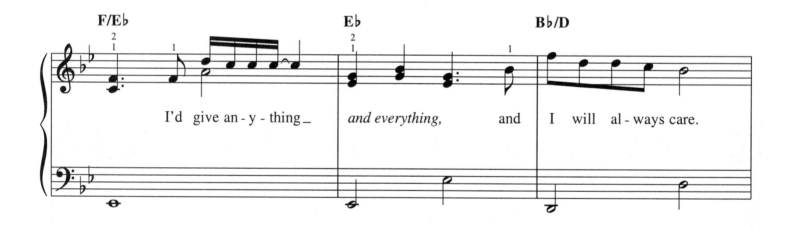

I'd give an - y - thing_   *and everything,*   and   I   will   al - ways care.

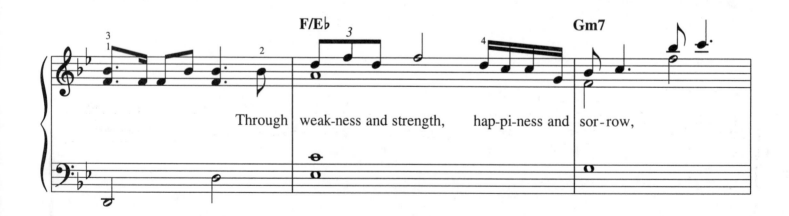

Through | weak-ness and strength,   hap-pi-ness and | sor-row,

Copyright © 1997 Songs Of PolyGram International, Inc., Loon Echo, Inc. and Out Of Pocket Productions Ltd.
All Rights on behalf of Out Of Pocket Productions Ltd. Controlled by Zomba Enterprises Inc. for the U.S. and Canada
International Copyright Secured   All Rights Reserved

for better, for worse,   I will love you with   ev - 'ry beat of my heart.

From this

Slowly

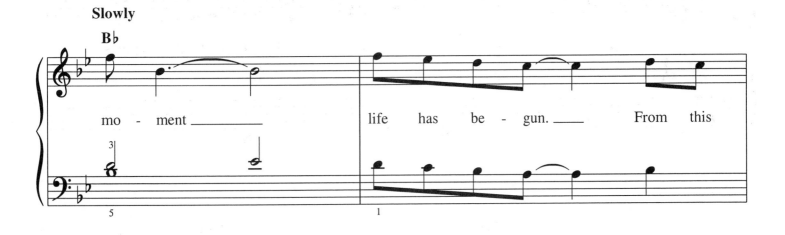

mo - ment _____   life has be - gun. _____   From this

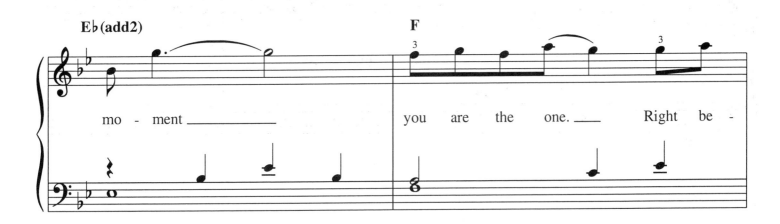

mo - ment _____   you are the one. _____   Right be -

side you   is   where I   be - long, _____

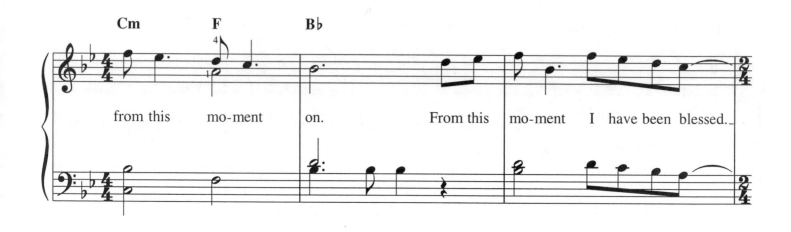

from this   mo-ment   on.   From this   mo-ment   I   have been blessed. __

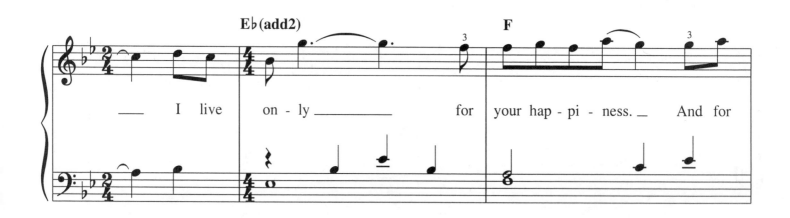

___   I   live   on - ly _____   for   your hap - pi - ness. __   And for

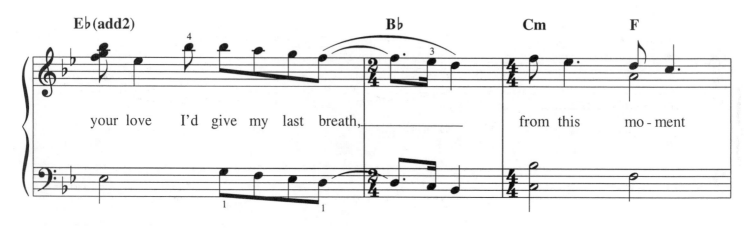

your love   I'd give my last breath, _____   from this   mo - ment

on.   I give my hand __ to you __ with all __ my

heart. _____ Can't wait to live __ my life __ with you, __ can't

wait to start. __   You and I ___ will nev - er be __ a -

part. _____ My dreams _____ came true _____ be -

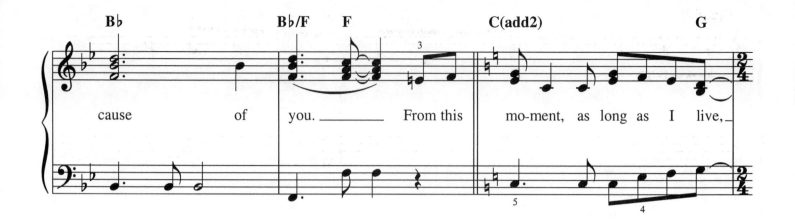

cause   of   you. _____ From this   mo-ment, as long as I live,_

_____ I will   love you, _____   I   prom-ise you this. _____   There is

noth - ing   I   would-n't   give, _____   from this   mo - ment

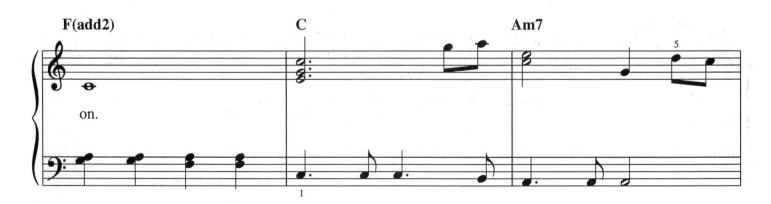

on.

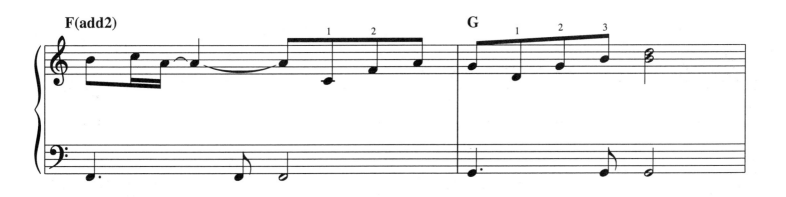

You're the rea - son I ___ be - lieve _ in love, _____ and

you're the an - swer to ___ my prayers _ from up a - bove. _

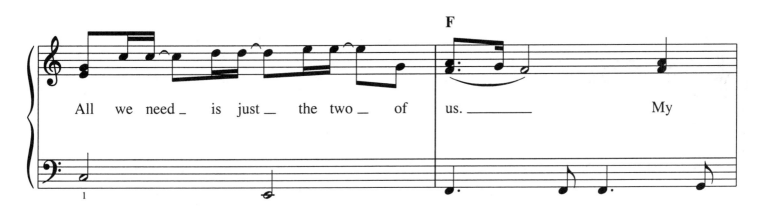

All we need _ is just _ the two _ of us. _____ My

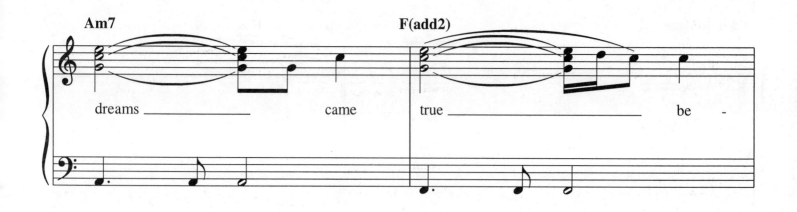

dreams _____ came true _____ be -

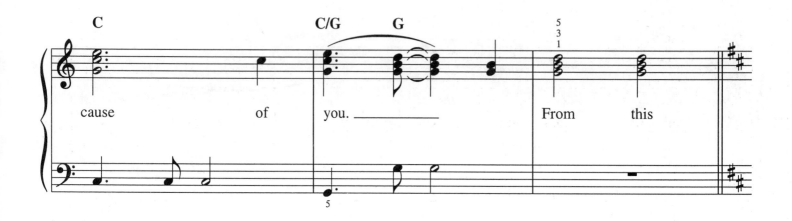

cause of you. _____ From this

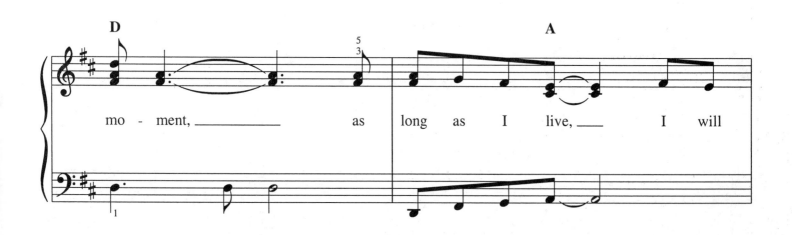

mo - ment, _____ as long as I live, _____ I will

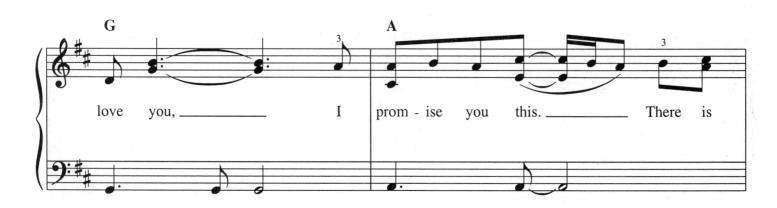

love you, _____ I prom - ise you this. _____ There is

noth - ing   I   would - n't   give,

from this   mo - ment.   I   will   love   you   as   long   as   I   live,

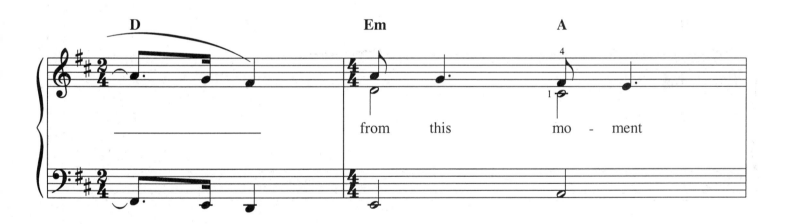

_____   from   this   mo - ment

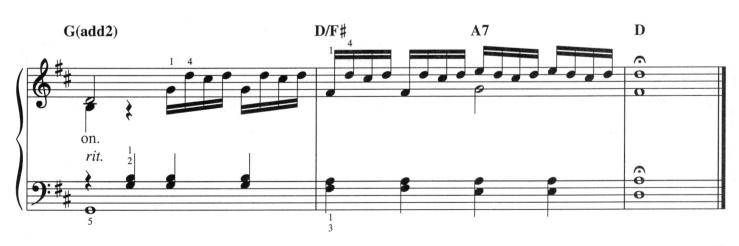

on.
rit.

(God Must Have Spent)
A Little More Time on You

Words and Music by Carl Sturken
and Evan Rogers

© Copyright 1998 by MUSIC CORPORATION OF AMERICA, INC. and BAYJUN BEAT MUSIC
All Rights Controlled and Administered by MUSIC CORPORATION OF AMERICA, INC.
International Copyright Secured   All Rights Reserved

__ how I feel? __ My life was com - plete. __ I
- es them all. __ More pre - cious than an - y

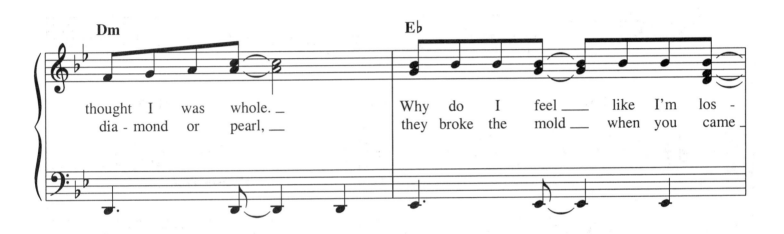

thought I was whole. __ Why do I feel __ like I'm los -
dia - mond or pearl, __ they broke the mold __ when you came

- ing con - trol? __ I nev - er (1.,3.) thought that love could feel __ like this, __
__ in this world. __ And I'm (2.) try - in' hard to fig - ure out __

and you changed my world with just __ one kiss. __
just how I ev - er did __ with - out __

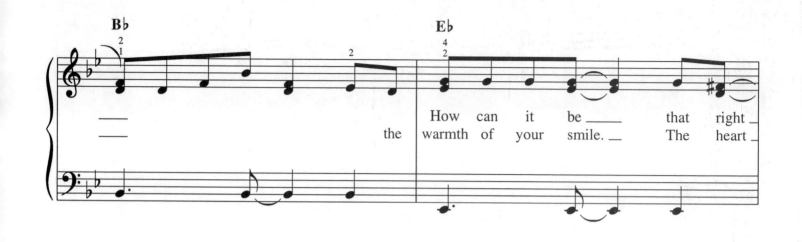

How can it be _____ that right
the warmth of your smile. _ The heart

_____ here with me _____ there's an an - gel? It's a
_____ of a child that's deep in - side _____ leaves me

mir - a - cle. _____
pur - i - fied. _____ Your love is like a riv - er,

peace - ful and deep. _ Your soul is like a se - cret that I

nev - er could keep. ____ When I look in - to your eyes I

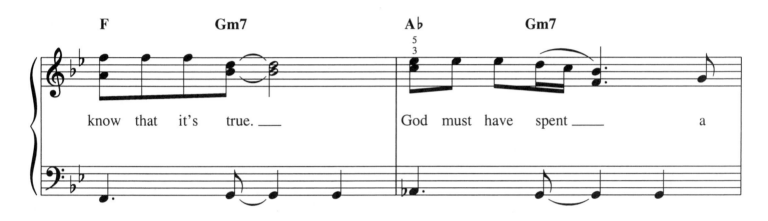

know that it's true. ____ God must have spent ____ a

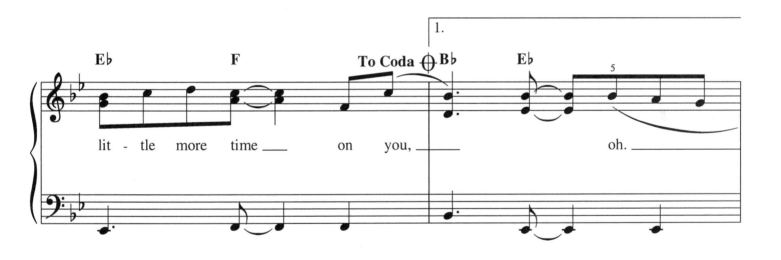

lit - tle more time ____ on you, ____ oh. ____

____ Lit - tle more time. ____

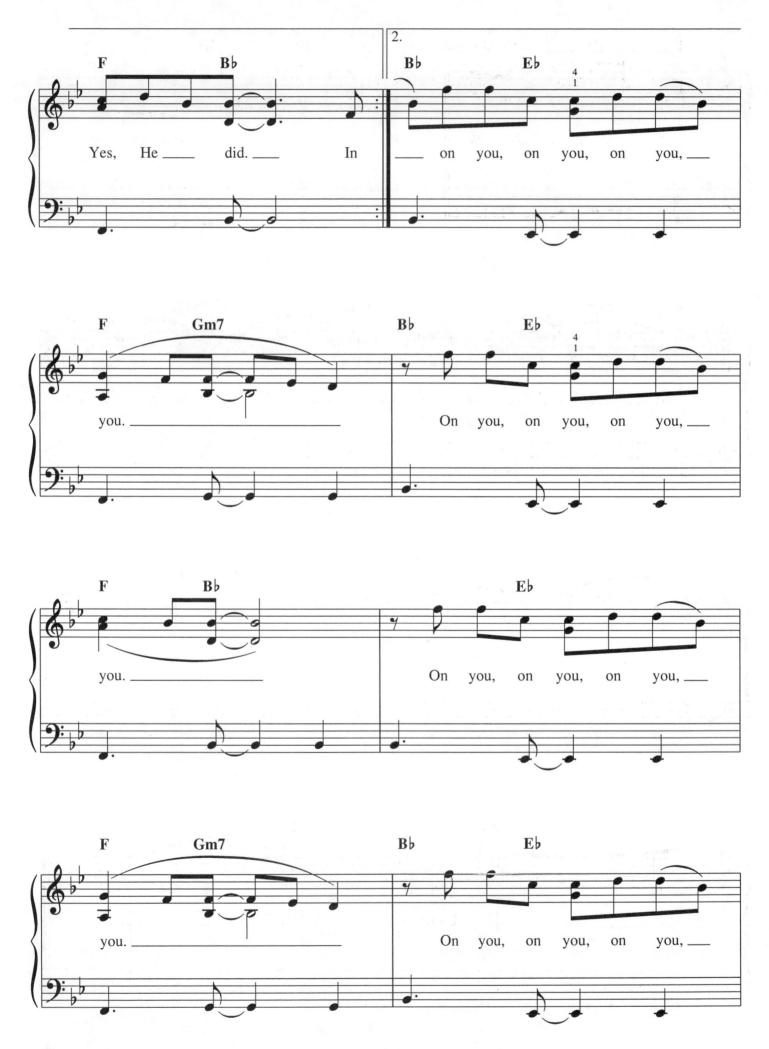

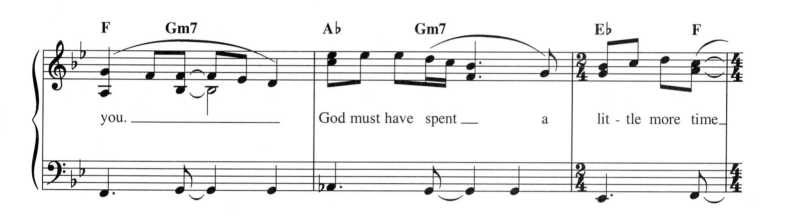

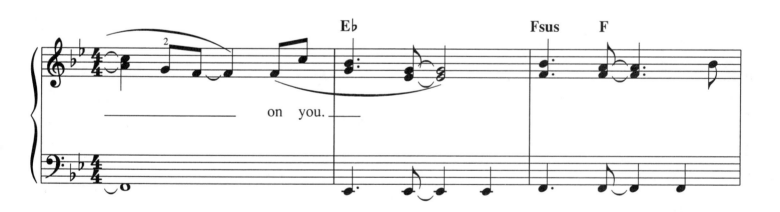

Hard Habit to Break

Words and Music by
John Lewis Parker and Stephen Kipner

© Copyright 1984 by MUSIC CORPORATION OF AMERICA, INC., EMI APRIL MUSIC INC. and STEPHEN A. KIPNER MUSIC
All Rights for STEPHEN A. KIPNER MUSIC Controlled and Administered by EMI APRIL MUSIC INC.
International Copyright Secured   All Rights Reserved

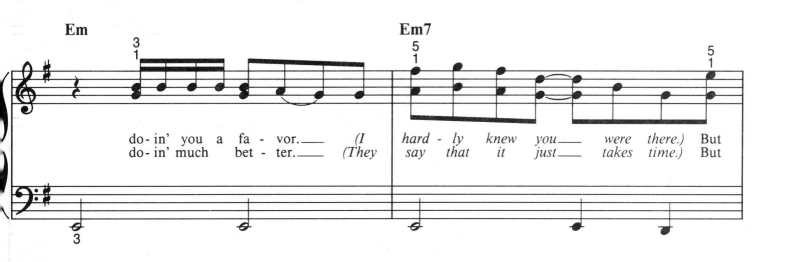

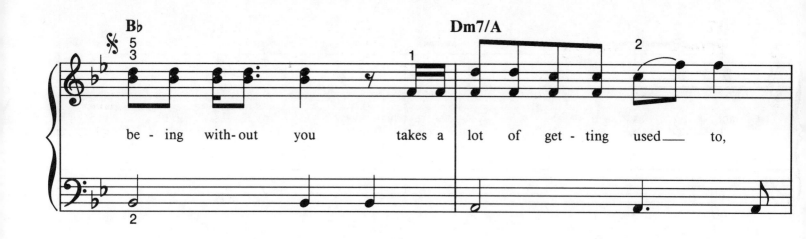

be - ing with-out you takes a lot of get - ting used ___ to,

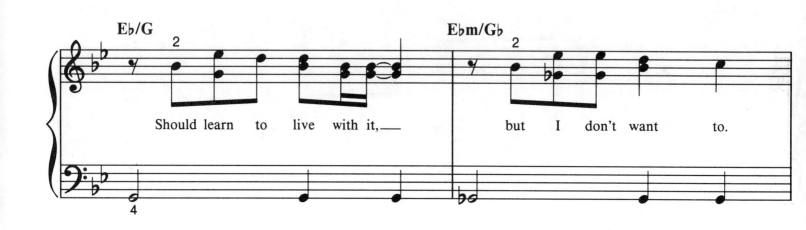

Should learn to live with it, ___ but I don't want to.

Be - ing with-out you is all a big mis - take, ___ In -

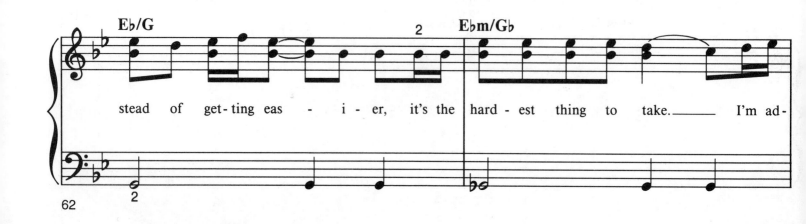

stead of get - ting eas - i - er, it's the hard - est thing to take. ___ I'm ad-

62

dict - ed to you, babe,___ you're a hard ha - bit to break.___

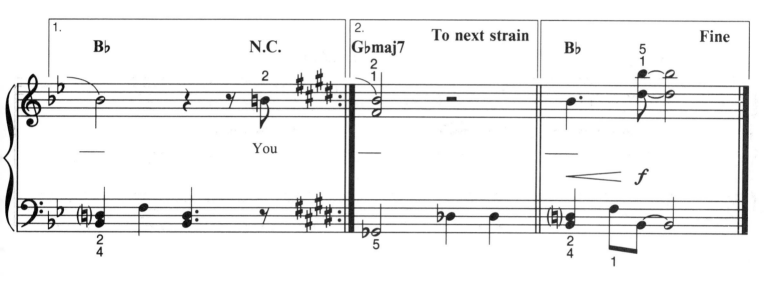

You — Can't go on, Just can't go on, on.

Can't go on, Just can't go on, on.

Can't go on, Just can't go on, on. Now

Have I Told You Lately

Words and Music by
Van Morrison

Copyright © 1989 Caledonia Publishing Ltd.
All Rights for the United States and Canada Administered by Songs Of PolyGram International, Inc.
International Copyright Secured   All Rights Reserved

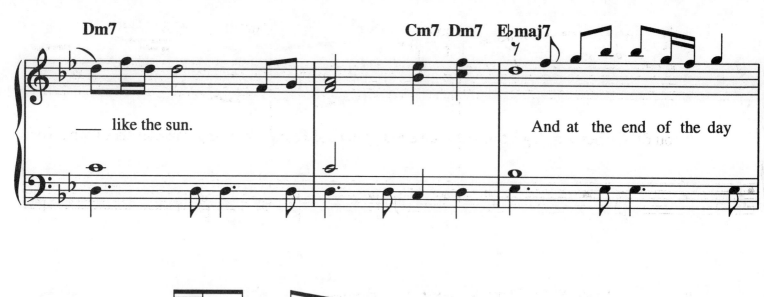

_____ like the sun.

And at the end of the day

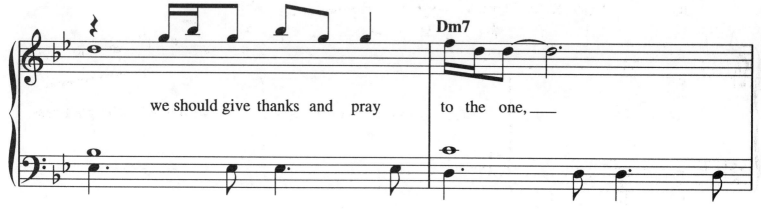

we should give thanks and pray

to the one, _____

to the one. _____ Have I

to the one. _____ And have I told you late-ly that I

love you? Have I told you there's no one else a - bove you? _____

If I Ever Fall in Love

Words and Music by
Carl Martin

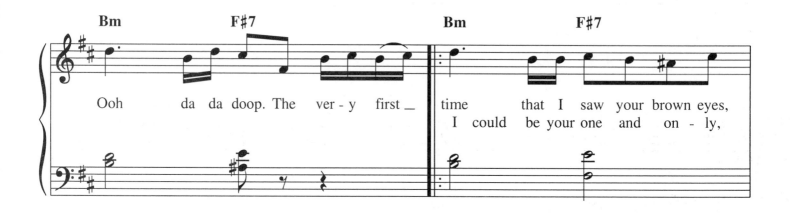

© Copyright 1992 by MUSIC CORPORATION OF AMERICA, INC., GASOLINE ALLEY MUSIC and CAMEO APPEARANCE BY RAMSES
All Rights Controlled and Administered by MUSIC CORPORATION OF AMERICA, INC.
International Copyright Secured   All Rights Reserved

one.   But I was | caught up   in phys-i - cal at - trac - tion,
need.

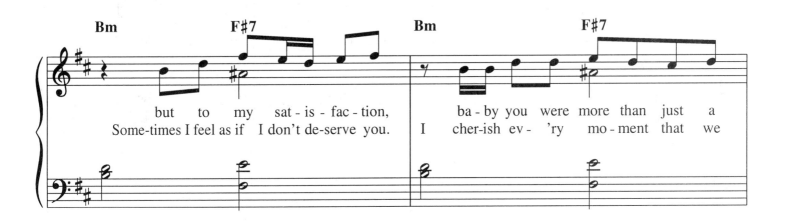

but to my sat - is - fac - tion,   ba - by you were more than just   a
Some-times I feel as if   I don't de-serve you.   I   cher-ish ev- 'ry   mo - ment that we

face. __ }   And   if   I   ev... ev - er   fall   in   love   a -
share. __ }

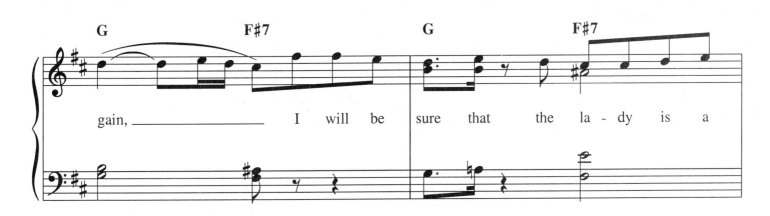

gain, _____   I will   be   sure   that   the   la - dy   is   a

friend. And if I ev... ev - er fall in love so

true, _____ I will be sure that the la - dy's just like you. _____ Oh.

Ooh da da doop da doop. Ooh da da doop do doop.

The ver - y next time she'll be my friend. If I say that

you. ___ My friend. Ver-y next time she will be my friend, some-one who I can be-lieve in.

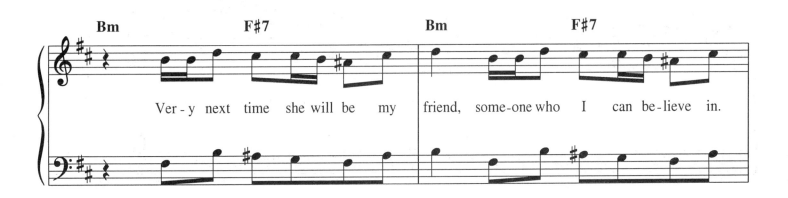

Ver - y next time she will be my friend, some-one who I can be-lieve in.

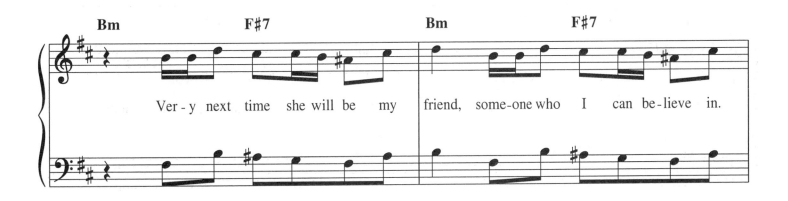

Ver - y next time she will be my friend, some-one who I can be-lieve in.

Ver-y next time she will be my friend. And if I

you. ___

Leaving on a Jet Plane

Words and Music by
John Denver

Copyright © 1967; Renewed 1995 Cherry Lane Music Publishing Company, Inc. (ASCAP) and DreamWorks Songs (ASCAP)
Worldwide Rights for DreamWorks Songs Administered by Cherry Lane Music Publishing Company, Inc.
International Copyright Secured   All Rights Reserved

You're Still the One

Words and Music by Shania Twain
and R.J. Lange

Copyright © 1997 Songs Of PolyGram International, Inc., Loon Echo, Inc. and Out Of Pocket Productions Ltd.
All Rights on behalf of Out Of Pocket Productions Ltd. Controlled by Zomba Enterprises Inc. for the U.S. and Canada
International Copyright Secured   All Rights Reserved

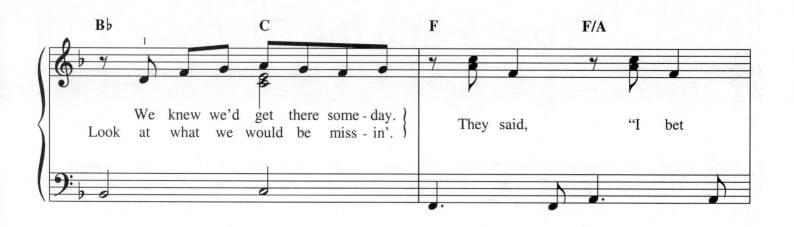

We knew we'd get there some-day.
Look at what we would be miss-in'.
They said, "I bet

they'll nev-er make it." But just look at us hold-ing on.

We're still to-geth-er, still go-ing strong.

(You're still the one.) You're still the one I run to,

the one that I be-long to. ___ You're still the one I want for life. (You're still the one.)___

To Coda ⊕

___You're still the one that I love, the on-ly one I dream of.___ You're still the one I kiss good -

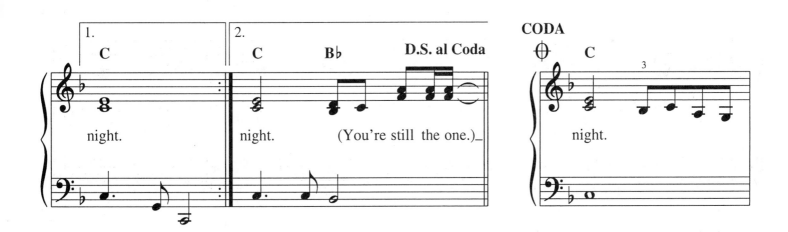

1.
C

night.

2.
C   B♭

night.   (You're still the one.)_

D.S. al Coda

CODA
⊕   C

night.

F   F/A   B♭   C

I'm so glad we made it.   Look how far we've come, my ba - by.___

77

Someone Like You
from JEKYLL & HYDE

Words by Leslie Bricusse
Music by Frank Wildhorn

Copyright © 1990, 1995 Stage & Screen Music, Ltd. (BMI), Cherry Lane Music Publishing Company, Inc. (ASCAP),
DreamWorks Songs (ASCAP), Les Etoiles De La Musique (ASCAP) and Scaramanga Music, Inc. (ASCAP)
Worldwide Rights for Stage & Screen Music, Ltd. Administered by Cherry River Music Co.
Worldwide Rights for DreamWorks Songs, Les Etoiles De La Musique and Scaramanga Music, Inc. Administered by Cherry Lane Music Publishing Company, Inc.
International Copyright Secured   All Rights Reserved

fly, but scared to try. But if

some - one like you found some - one like me, then

sud - den - ly noth - ing would ev - er be the same! My

heart would take wing—— and I'd feel so a - live,—— if

some - one like you—— found me!

rit.   a tempo

D.S. al Coda

Coda

80

Sunshine on My Shoulders

Words by John Denver
Music by John Denver, Mike Taylor and Dick Kniss

Copyright © 1971; Renewed 1999 Cherry Lane Music Publishing Company, Inc. (ASCAP) and DreamWorks Songs (ASCAP)
Worldwide Rights for DreamWorks Songs Administered by Cherry Lane Music Publishing Company, Inc.
International Copyright Secured   All Rights Reserved

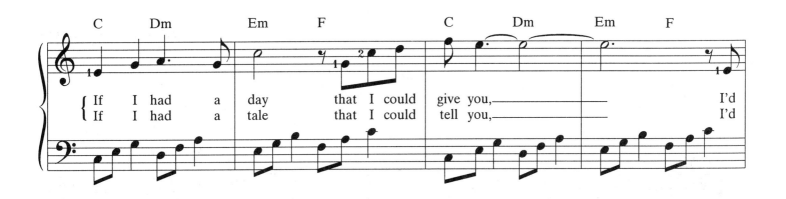

If I had a day that I could give you,— I'd
If I had a tale that I could tell you,— I'd

give to you a day just like to - day.—
tell a tale sure to make you smile.—

2nd time, D.C. al Fine

If I had a song that I could sing for you,— I'd
If I had a wish that I could wish for you,— I'd

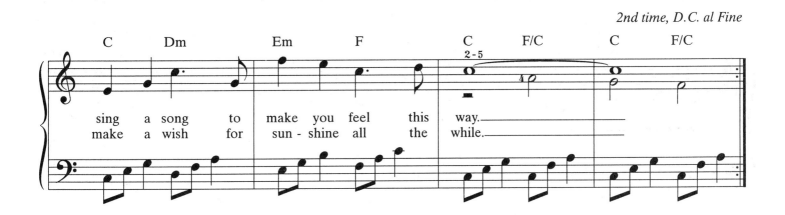

sing a song to make you feel this way.—
make a wish for sun - shine all the while.—

When You Say Nothing at All

Words and Music by Don Schlitz
and Paul Overstreet

Moderately Slow

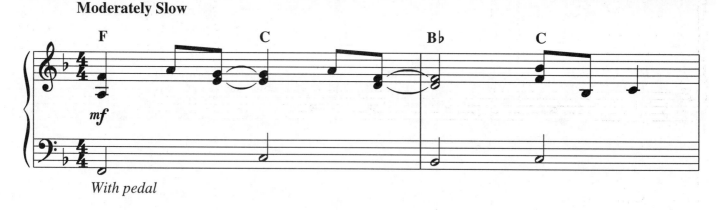

With pedal

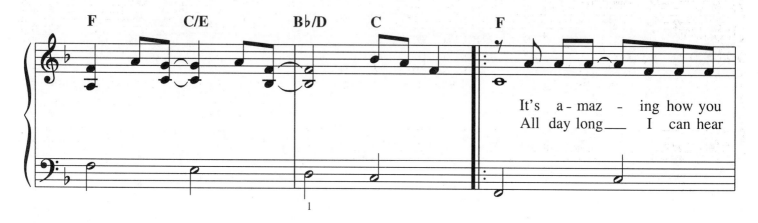

It's a - maz - ing how you
All day long___ I can hear

can speak right___ to my heart___
peo - ple talk - ing out loud.___

With - out say - ing a word___ you can light up the dark.___
But when you___ hold me near___ you drown out the crowd.___

© Copyright 1988 by MCA MUSIC PUBLISHING, A Division of UNIVERSAL STUDIOS, INC.,
DON SCHLITZ MUSIC, SCREEN GEMS-EMI MUSIC INC. and SCARLET MOON MUSIC
All Rights for DON SCHLITZ MUSIC Controlled and Administered by MCA MUSIC PUBLISHING, A Division of UNIVERSAL STUDIOS, INC.
All Rights for SCARLET MOON MUSIC Administered by COPYRIGHT MANAGEMENT INTERNATIONAL, LLC
International Copyright Secured   All Rights Reserved

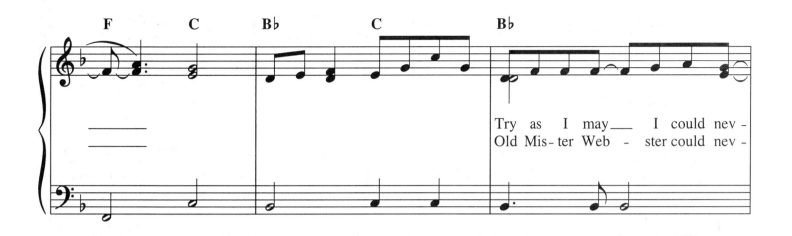

Try as I may___ I could nev -
Old Mis - ter Web - ster could nev -

- er ex-plain___ what I hear___ when you don't___ say a thing.
- er de - fine___ what's be - ing said___ be-tween your___ heart and mine.

The smile on your face lets me know___

___ that you need___ me. There's a truth in your eyes say - ing you'll___

_____ nev - er leave _____ me. A touch of your hand _____ says you'll catch

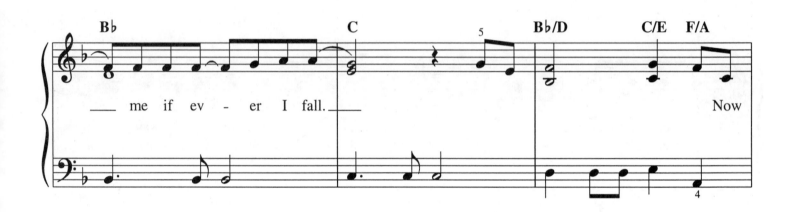

_____ me if ev - er I fall. _____ Now

you say it best _____ when you say noth-ing at all. _____

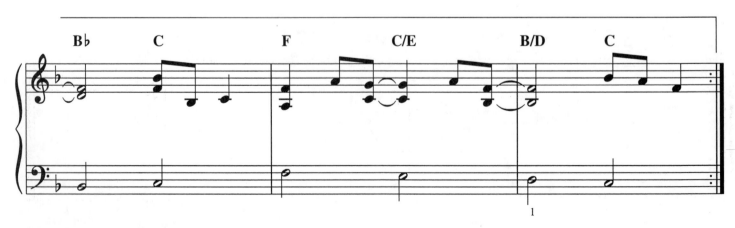

when you say noth - ing at all.

D.S. al Coda

The

CODA

when you say noth-ing at all.

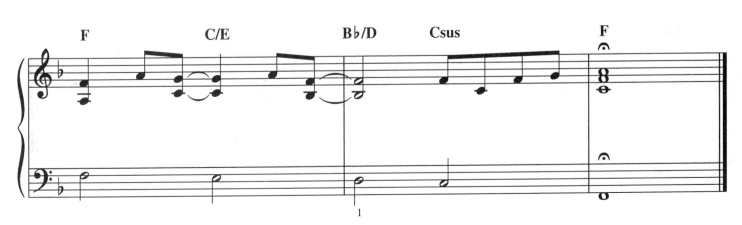